DANIEL'S
PROPHECIES
OF COVENANT
CHANGE

DANIEL'S
PROPHECIES
OF COVENANT
CHANGE

*Understanding Daniel's
Visions of the Future*

BILL SAXTON

REDEMPTION◆PRESS

Published by Redemption Press, PO Box 427, Enumclaw, WA 98022

ISBN 13 (Print): 978-1-63232-304-0
ISBN 13 (eBook): 978-1-63232-305-7
Library of Congress Catalog Card Number: 2013906320

CONTENTS

PREFACE

IKE MOST EVANGELICAL Christians of the late twentieth century, I was led to assume that the prophetic scenarios of the "end times" as laid out by authors such as Hal Lindsey, and more recently, by Tim LaHaye and Jerry Jenkins in their *Left Behind* book series, were the best and only way of understanding those prophetic passages of the Bible that looked beyond the New Testament events. In studying the Bible myself, however, I struggled with many passages for which this approach seemed to be problematic. Furthermore, as someone concerned with defending the reliability of Scripture, I was not totally comfortable with their proposed answers to the cynics and skeptics who concluded that Jesus and Paul were false teachers because some of the things they predicted apparently didn't ever happen.

Eventually I became acquainted with a different understanding of these prophetic passages of Scripture, which took more seriously both the historical context of the New Testament writers and their original readers, and the use of Old Testament imagery by Jesus and the New Testament writers. This view, commonly called the "preterist" (meaning "in the past") perspective, contends that most of these prophetic passages, properly understood, describe and were actually fulfilled in the events of the first century, which culminated in the destruction of the temple in Jerusalem in AD 70. I believe the key to this understanding is found in the basic transition from the world of the Old Testament to the transformed world made possible by the Lord Jesus Christ.

New World, New Reality

The Bible consists of two parts, commonly called the Old Testament and the New Testament. These two testaments tell the story of the fundamental "covenant" relationship between God and humans as it developed and changed throughout history, with the Old Testament as the written record of the development of this "old covenant" relationship prior to the coming of Jesus, and the New Testament being the record of the establishment of a new and better "new covenant" relationship established by Jesus.

While there is a basic continuity between the old covenant and the new covenant, we also need to appreciate the radical differences between the covenants. The writer of the book of Hebrews in the New Testament focuses on this contrast, comparing the old and new covenants and showing how the new covenant is superior in every way.

We are far enough removed from Old Testament life that perhaps we don't readily appreciate the radical change in thinking and lifestyle that the new covenant in Jesus involved. Consider first, how life in relation to God changed for Gentiles (non-Jews). The story of the book of Acts traces the gradual realization by the early disciples that the good news of forgiveness and new life through Jesus could apply to Gentiles as well as to Jews. What a change! Now Gentiles could be included in God's family through Jesus without becoming Jews—without circumcision being required for men, without making animal sacrifices at the temple, and without taking on all the obligations of the Law of Moses. No longer was there to be a wall of separation between clean and unclean things, between clean and unclean foods, and between Jew and Gentile.

For Jews, the changes would be even more momentous, though it did not initially seem so. Consider this: God invaded our world in the incarnation when Jesus was born in Bethlehem, yet for some thirty to thirty-five years, only a small number of people—Joseph, Mary, a few shepherds, some "wise men from the East," and a few others—realized that anything of any significance had happened. Life went on as usual. Likewise, when Jesus died for our sins, only a small but growing group of disciples believed He was the Messiah and appreciated the importance of His death for them. For another thirty-five or so years, life for Jews who rejected Jesus went on as before, with a life centered on the calendar cycles of sabbaths and special pilgrimage festivals to the temple, obedience to the Law of Moses, trying to avoid any ritual uncleanness, and the need for the atoning animal sacrifices at the temple in Jerusalem, until the temple was destroyed in AD 70. After that, life for the Jews would never be the same. Since sacrifices were only allowed at the temple, their only means of atonement was gone. Jews were now forced to either acknowledge Jesus as Messiah or redefine their religion without a temple (resulting in modern-day Judaism, which is centered on those parts of the Law and their traditions not involving the temple and sacrifices). For the followers of Jesus, the destruction of the temple was dramatic proof that Jesus's death on the cross had replaced the animal sacrifices at the temple, and was the previously unthinkable fulfillment of His prediction that the temple would be destroyed in that generation.

In this study of Daniel I try to show that the prophecies of Daniel are most understandable when seen "covenant-ally," as pointing to the end of the old covenant era and the establishment of the new covenant in Jesus. This analysis of Daniel's prophecies also is consistent with, and supports, a preterist understanding of other prophetic passages that focus on this period of covenant change, such as the Mount of Olives Discourse (Matt. 24 and parallels in Mark and Luke) and most of the book of Revelation.

—Bill Saxton

INTRODUCTION

Structure of the Book of Daniel

BEFORE LOOKING AT the individual prophecies in the book of Daniel, it is important to appreciate the structure of the book as a whole. Three aspects of the overall structure are particularly noteworthy.

First, the book can be readily divided in half based on the subject matter. Chapters 1–6 have been described as "court narratives," recounting some key events in the life of Daniel and his three Jewish friends—Shadrach, Meshach, and Abednego—during their captivity in Babylon. Added to them in chapters 7–12, are Daniel's accounts of the revelations he personally received (beyond the interpretation of King Nebuchadnezzar's dream, which was given to Daniel as recorded in Dan. 2).

Additionally, Daniel can also be divided based on the language in which the original text was written. Daniel 1:1–2:3

was written in Hebrew, while Daniel 2:4–7:28 was written in Aramaic (the common language of that area of the world at that time). Then Daniel 8:1–12:13 was again written in Hebrew. These linguistic changes signal a significant difference in focus for these sections.

Thus, the middle section (Dan. 2–7) spotlights God's ultimate sovereignty over the kingdoms of the world and their rulers, with Nebuchadnezzar and Belshazzar personally being confronted with this truth. The cohesive nature of this section is additionally apparent in the chiastic structure (ABCCBA) that frames chapters 2–7. In this analysis,

A = chapters 2 and 7, which give panoramic views of the present and future kingdoms and of God's ultimate kingdom being established;

B = chapters 3 and 6, which give parallel demonstrations of God's sovereign care for His people, in the accounts of the fiery furnace and the lions' den;

C = chapters 4 and 5, which show God's judgment of arrogant rulers.

The passages of Daniel written in Hebrew (Dan. 1:1–2:4; 8:1–12:13), in contrast, focus specifically on God's covenant people and place (the temple, Jerusalem, and the Promised Land). Thus, we find that the visions received by Daniel in chapters 8–12 are previewing the fall and rise of kingdoms specifically in relation to the Jews, their land, and their temple in Jerusalem. As we will see, this covenantal focus helps significantly in understanding the details of all of the prophecies as being intended to speak to the change of covenants brought about in Christ Jesus.

Overview of the Prophecies in Daniel

In the book of Daniel, two dreams/visions are given to King Nebuchadnezzar and interpreted by Daniel. The dream of chapter 4 is a message specifically directed to Nebuchadnezzar personally, and is fulfilled in his lifetime. The dream of chapter 2, however, is given in response to King Nebuchadnezzar's pondering of the future and carries far beyond his lifetime.

The thesis of this work is that this latter dream-prophecy of chapter 2 and all of those prophecies of the future given to Daniel in chapters 7–12, are interconnected, revealing various aspects of the end of the old covenant era and the establishment of the new covenant and the kingdom of God in Jesus. Each prophecy ends at the time of the covenant change events: the establishment of the new covenant through the incarnation, life, atoning death, resurrection, ascension, and heavenly enthronement of the Lord Jesus Christ, and the formal end of the old covenant with the judgment on rebellious Israel and the destruction of the Jewish temple in AD 70.

Together, these five prophecies (Dan. 2; 7; 8; 9; 10–12) provide a fivefold lens on the same sequence of events. As the revelations unfold, the future is increasingly revealed to Daniel in greater historical detail, with an increasing sharpness of focus on the transitional events involved in the change of covenants.

Thus, in the chapter 2 dream-vision given to Nebuchadnezzar of the four-part statue, the focus is on the kingdom of God, which would conquer other kingdoms and ultimately be established and endure forever. A main theme of Jesus' teaching was of this kingdom of God, which was being established in Him.

In the parallel dream-vision of the four beasts in chapter 7, the heavenly court sits in judgment on the four kingdoms, the "son of man" is enthroned as King of all Kings, and the saints inherit the kingdom. Jesus' most common self-identification, of course, was as "Son of Man," with all this background behind it.

The prophecy recorded in chapter 8 begins with a ram and a goat, but ultimately focuses on "the time of the end." This time of the end, as will be shown, refers to the end of the old covenant era, comprised of the time from its beginning under Herod the Great to its culmination at the destruction of the Jewish temple.

The seventy "weeks" of Daniel 9 regarding Jerusalem, span the time frame from Daniel's day to the end of the old covenant, highlighting the Messiah's establishment of the new and better covenant, His destruction of the temple, and the ending of the old covenant animal sacrifices.

The last prophecy, in Daniel 10–12, provides a more detailed description of the events in the period from Daniel's time to the end of the old covenant age, culminating in the resurrection of the dead and their final judgment.

Chapter 1

DANIEL 2: THE ESTABLISHMENT OF
THE KINGDOM OF GOD

NEBUCHADNEZZAR'S DREAM IN Daniel 2 is explained by Daniel as follows:

To you, O king, as you lay in bed came thoughts of what would be after this, and he who reveals mysteries made known to you what is to be. But as for me, this mystery has been revealed to me, not because of any wisdom that I have more than all the living, but in order that the interpretation may be made known to the king, and that you may know the thoughts of your mind.

You saw, O king, and behold, a great image. This image, mighty and of exceeding brightness, stood before you, and its appearance was frightening. The head of this image was of fine gold, its chest and arms of silver, its middle and thighs of bronze, its legs of iron, its feet partly of iron and partly of clay. As you looked, a stone was cut out by no human hand, and it struck the image on its feet of iron and clay, and broke them in pieces.

Then the iron, the clay, the bronze, the silver, and the gold, all together were broken in pieces, and became like the chaff of the summer threshing floors; and the wind carried them away, so that not a trace of them could be found. But the stone that struck the image became a great mountain and filled the whole earth.

This was the dream. Now we will tell the king its interpretation. You, O king, the king of kings, to whom the God of heaven has given the kingdom, the power, and the might, and the glory, and into whose hand he has given, wherever they dwell, the children of man, the beasts of the field, and the birds of the heavens, making you rule over them all—you are the head of gold. Another kingdom inferior to you shall arise after you, and yet a third kingdom of bronze, which shall rule over all the earth. And there shall be a fourth kingdom, strong as iron, because iron breaks to pieces and shatters all things. And like iron that crushes, it shall break and crush all these. And as you saw the feet and toes, partly of potter's clay and partly of iron, it shall be a divided kingdom, but some of the firmness of iron shall be in it, just as you saw iron mixed with the soft clay. And as the toes of the feet were partly iron and partly clay, so the kingdom shall be partly strong and partly brittle. As you saw the iron mixed with soft clay, so they will mix with one another in marriage, but they will not hold together, just as iron does not mix with clay. And in the days of those kings the God of heaven will set up a kingdom that shall never be destroyed, nor shall the kingdom be left to another people. It shall break in pieces all these kingdoms and bring them to an end, and it shall stand forever, just as you saw that a stone was cut from a mountain by no human hand, and that it broke in pieces the iron, the bronze, the clay, the silver, and the gold. A great God has made known to the king what shall be after this. The dream is certain, and its interpretation sure.

(Dan. 2:29–45)

The Identities of the Four Kingdoms

The identities of the four kingdoms that comprise the statue in the dream interpreted by Daniel are clear.[1] Nebuchadnezzar's kingdom of Babylon (the head of gold) would eventually be conquered by the Medo-Persian Empire (the chest and arms of silver), which would in turn be conquered by Alexander the Great and the Greeks (the belly and thighs of bronze). The remnants of the Greek rule would in turn be swallowed up by the Roman Empire (the legs of iron and feet of iron and clay).

The statue's elements represent well these four successive kingdoms. Babylon was famous for its lavish use of gold. Its dominance preceded the development of silver coinage, which was used in paying the large mercenary army of their conquerors, the Medes and Persians. Then there is a distinctive historical association of bronze with the Greek world, and bronze was the preferred metal of the Greeks for military use. The armor of the Greek armies was bronze, and the famous Greek fighting ship, the trireme, had a bronze-plated prow and a large bronze battering ram extending beyond the prow. Finally, iron is appropriate to represent the Romans, as the Roman army was the first to extensively use iron on its warships, armor, and weaponry.[2]

Other associations between gold, silver, bronze, and iron are also noteworthy. First, they represent a declining monetary value per unit of weight. Symbolically, this may also suggest a decline in the absolute political power of the king, with Nebuchadnezzar having no challenge to his absolute authority over his kingdom, while Darius was restricted by his own need to submit to "the law of the Medes and the Persians" (Dan. 6:8–15). The Greek rulers represented a coalition of city-states, and the Greek "political tradition was more republican than its predecessor."[3] After them, the emperors of Rome had to deal with the Roman senate and the restrictions of Roman law, as well as the inherent weakness involved in giving their large Jewish minority a special status, with a great deal of independence in running their own affairs.

Conversely, however, these metals also have an increasing functional usefulness and strength. Also, they reflect an increasing availability. Natural resources of gold are seemingly less than those of silver, which are less plentiful than the copper and tin comprising bronze, which in turn are less than the abundance of natural iron ore. Finally, these factors may also suggest the successively greater geographical scope of the four kingdoms at the greatest geographical extent of their power.

So the four kingdoms are readily apparent. But an immediate question may spring to mind: Why these four kingdoms, and only these four? What about contemporaneous kingdoms in other parts of the world, or other kingdoms that came after these four in history? The answer: The focus on these four kingdoms, and only these four, must be understood in regard to the Bible's focus on the covenant promises of God that were being worked out in the descendants of Abraham, Isaac, and Jacob. These four kingdoms are the ruling powers that, beginning with King Nebuchadnezzar of Babylon, one after another, would control the Lord's covenant people and the place at the center of those promises—"the glorious land" of the Jews (Dan. 8:9; 11:16, 41), Jerusalem, and the Jewish temple. This helps in understanding, for example, the description of the third kingdom as one that "shall rule over all the earth" (2:39), whereby "all the earth" represents that area of the world relationally involved with God's covenant people. Similarly, the same Greek word used here (*oikoumene*) in the Septuagint Greek translation of Daniel commonly used in Jesus's day, is found in the New Testament to refer to the extent of the Roman Empire, in which God's people and place resided (cf. Luke 2:1; Acts 11:28).

Feet of Iron and Clay

The Roman Empire is further described as having legs of iron and "feet and toes, partly of potter's clay and partly of iron." Daniel explains that this represents "a divided kingdom," which "will be partly strong and partly brittle," and that "as you saw the iron mixed with soft clay, so they will mix with one another in marriage, but they will not hold together, just as iron does not mix with clay." How are we to understand this? Though the reference is ambiguous, one intriguing possibility is that the clay represents the Jewish people. At least two biblical passages suggest this connection: Isaiah 64:8 ("But now, O LORD, you are our

Father; we are the clay, and you are our potter; we are all the work of your hand") and Jeremiah 18:6b ("O house of Israel, can I not do with you as this potter has done? declares the LORD. Behold, like the clay in the potter's hand, so are you in my hand, O house of Israel"). Two additional factors support this possibility. The Jews were a large minority spread out throughout much of the Roman Empire, with the Jews estimated to have constituted as much as one tenth of the total population.[4] In addition, the Jews had a unique legal position within Roman society, whereby the Jews administered their own judicial affairs among themselves in regard to almost any matter except capital punishment, and were excused from supporting and participating in the common honorific worship of the Roman gods. The "marriage" of the Jews and Romans would not last, as the clay of Israel would not mix with the iron of Rome.

It is also noteworthy that the clay becomes partly "brittle" (Dan. 2:42), suggesting it is already hardened into a final form and no longer malleable by the Potter. As a reference to Israel this brings to mind the teachings of Jesus about the new unshrunk cloth that would not work to patch an old garment, and about the new wine that should not be put into old hardened wineskins (cf. Mark 2:21–22). The new covenant of Jesus would not be limited by the old cloth, the old, wineskins, of the old covenant. Likewise, the reference in Daniel 2:33–35 to the "brittle" clay—which would be broken to pieces and blown away by the wind, along with iron, bronze, silver, and gold—points to the formal end of obsolete old covenant Israel once the new covenant would be established (cf. Heb. 8:13).

The Establishment of the Kingdom of God

During the fourth (Roman) kingdom, a rock is "cut out by no human hand." It strikes the statue on its feet and brings all the kingdoms to an end at the same time. The rock then grows into a mountain that fills the whole earth. Daniel explains to King Nebuchadnezzar that this rock/mountain symbolizes the kingdom that God will establish during the rule of the fourth (Roman) Empire and that will endure forever.

When we turn to the gospel accounts, we find this being fulfilled. Jesus begins His ministry with "the kingdom of God is at hand" (Mark 1:15) and makes the kingdom of God a dominant theme of His teaching. His kingdom was being established and would grow, like yeast spreading through the whole loaf and like the small mustard seed growing to be the largest of garden plants (Matt. 13:31–33). The rock "cut out by no human hand," from which the kingdom of God grows, is Jesus.

The "mountain" imagery pointing to Jesus and His reign in the lives of His followers is also found in the prophecy of Isaiah 2:1–4:

> The word that Isaiah the son of Amoz saw concerning Judah and Jerusalem. It shall come to pass in the latter days that the mountain of the house of the LORD shall be established as the highest of the mountains, and shall be lifted up above the hills; and all the nations shall flow to it, and many peoples shall come, and say: "Come, let us go up to the mountain of the LORD, to the house of the God of Jacob, that he may teach us his ways and that

we may walk in his paths." For out of Zion shall go the law, and the word of the LORD from Jerusalem. He shall judge between the nations, and shall decide disputes for many peoples; and they shall beat their swords into plowshares, and their spears into pruning hooks; nation shall not lift up sword against nation, neither shall they learn war anymore.

The writer of Hebrews further identifies this rock/mountain when he states that Christians "have come to Mount Zion and to the city of the living God, the heavenly Jerusalem" (Heb. 12:22). Not the literal earthly Mount Zion and Jerusalem, but the heavenly city of God.

But in what way did the kingdom of God crush these four kingdoms and sweep them away during the time of the Roman Empire? If we think of these kingdoms in physical, earthly terms we will miss the point. However, if we appreciate the spiritual forces behind these kingdoms we find our answer.

By His atoning death on the cross and resurrection, Jesus conquered sin and death, once and for all time. He ascended to the Father and is enthroned now. The kingdom of Jesus involves "all authority in heaven and on earth" (Matt. 28:18). He is seated "far above all rule and authority and power and dominion" (Eph. 1:20–21), with "the name that is above every name" (Phil. 2:9). By the power of His Spirit He is overcoming the spiritual forces behind all earthly kingdoms. The kingdom of God has been established and, though not yet fully experienced, is gradually conquering through the sacrificial preaching of the good news, resulting in the transformed lives of more and more people surrendered to His kingship. The time for the peoples of the world to live in ignorance, dominated by other "gods," is over. As Paul told the people of Athens in Acts 17:24–31, "the times of ignorance God overlooked, but now he commands all people everywhere to repent" prior to their judgment by the Lord Jesus.

No longer are there such political entities as the Babylonian, Persian, Greek, and Roman empires. But also, and more importantly in this context, the spiritual forces that dominated them are also long gone, whether the gods of Babylon and Persia, the Greco-Roman pantheon of gods, or their leaders' claims to divinity.

Also, there is that significant implication that the clay in this dream represents God's Old Testament covenant people Israel. The clay was also crushed and swept away by the wind when the rock/mountain of the kingdom of God was established (vv. 35, 45)! Thus, the Jews would see the end of their unique covenant relationship with God when their temple would be destroyed in AD 70 (cf. Heb. 8:13; Matt. 21:43–45). In the establishment of the kingdom of God and God's new covenant with humankind including both Jews and Gentiles, the old covenant between God and His people is swept away, along with the spiritual forces of "gods and goddesses" behind all of those four former empires.

Note that the dream stops with the establishment of the kingdom of God. That is all Nebuchadnezzar needed to know. The intent of this dream was fulfilled—to reveal to King Nebuchadnezzar the future establishment of the kingdom of God and to humble him before Daniel's God, the "God of heaven" and King above all kings.

In Daniel 2, Daniel is a young man (604 BC). Daniel must now wait until he is an old man, some fifty years later, to receive the prophecies of Daniel 7; 8; 9; and 10–12 (553–536 BC), which would clarify and expand the revelations. These later prophecies would be given to Daniel for him alone to know and record, not to be spoken of by him at that time to others. They would become more fully understandable only with the coming of Christ and the unfolding of the events connected to establishing the new covenant.

Chapter 2

DANIEL 7: THE SON OF MAN AND KINGS OF THE BEAST

In the first year of Belshazzar king of Babylon, Daniel saw a dream and visions of his head as he lay in his bed. Then he wrote down the dream and told the sum of the matter. Daniel declared, "I saw in my vision by night, and behold, the four winds of heaven were stirring up the great sea. And four great beasts came up out of the sea, different from one another. The first was like a lion and had eagles' wings. Then as I looked its wings were plucked off, and it was lifted up from the ground and made to stand on two feet like a man, and the mind of a man was given to it. And behold, another beast, a second one, like a bear. It was raised up on one side. It had three ribs in its mouth between its teeth; and it was told, 'Arise, devour much flesh.' After this I looked, and behold, another, like a leopard, with four wings of a bird on its back. And the beast had four heads, and dominion was given to it. After this I saw in the night visions, and behold, a fourth beast, terrifying and dreadful and exceedingly strong. It had great iron teeth; it devoured and broke in pieces and stamped what was left with its feet. It was different from all the beasts that were before it, and it had ten horns. I considered the horns, and behold, there came up among them another horn, a little one, before which three of the first horns were plucked up by the roots. And behold, in this horn were eyes like the eyes of a man, and a mouth speaking great things.

"As I looked, thrones were placed, and the Ancient of Days took his seat; his clothing was white as snow, and the hair of his head like pure wool; his throne was fiery flames; its wheels were burning fire. A stream of fire issued and came out from before him; a thousand thousands served him, and ten thousand times ten thousand stood before him; the court sat in judgment, and the books were opened.

"I looked then because of the sound of the great words that the horn was speaking. And as I looked, the beast was killed, and its body destroyed and given over to be burned with fire. As for the rest of the beasts, their dominion was taken away, but their lives were prolonged for a season and a time.

"I saw in the night visions, and behold, with the clouds of heaven there came one like a son of man, and he came to the Ancient of Days and was presented before him. And to him was given dominion and glory and a kingdom, that all peoples, nations, and languages should serve him; his dominion is an everlasting dominion, which shall not pass away, and his kingdom one that shall not be destroyed.

"As for me, Daniel, my spirit within me was anxious, and the visions of my head alarmed me. I approached one of those who stood there and asked him the truth concerning all this. So he told me and made known to me the interpretation of the things. 'These four great beasts are four kings who shall arise out of the earth. But the saints of the Most High shall receive the kingdom and possess the kingdom forever, forever and ever.'

"Then I desired to know the truth about the fourth beast, which was different from all the rest, exceedingly terrifying, with its teeth of iron and claws of bronze, and which devoured and broke in pieces and stamped what was left with its feet, and about the ten horns that were on its head, and the other horn that came up and before which three of them fell, the horn that had eyes and a mouth that spoke great things, and that seemed greater than its companions. As I looked, this horn made war with the saints and prevailed over them, until the Ancient of Days came, and judgment was given for the saints of the Most High, and the time came when the saints possessed the kingdom.

"Thus he said: 'As for the fourth beast, there shall be a fourth kingdom on earth, which shall be different from all the kingdoms, and it shall devour the whole earth, and trample it down, and break it to pieces. As for the ten horns, out of this kingdom ten kings shall arise, and another shall arise after them; he shall be different from the former ones, and shall put down three kings. He shall speak words against the Most High, and shall wear out the saints of the Most High, and shall think to change the times and the law; and they shall be given into his hand for a time, times, and half a time. But the court shall sit in judgment, and his dominion shall be taken away, to be consumed and destroyed to the end.

And the kingdom and the dominion and the greatness of the kingdoms under the whole heaven shall be given to the people of the saints of the Most High; his kingdom shall be an everlasting kingdom, and all dominions shall serve and obey him.'

"Here is the end of the matter. As for me, Daniel, my thoughts greatly alarmed me, and my color changed, but I kept the matter in my heart."

—Daniel 7:1–28

Introduction

THE FIRST PROPHECY (in chapter 2) had come to Nebuchadnezzar as a dream and was subsequently revealed to Daniel with its interpretation. Its focus was on God's message specifically to Nebuchadnezzar in response to his "thoughts of what would be after this" (2:29), graciously revealing to him the future establishment of God's kingdom. In chapter 4, Nebuchadnezzar is given another dream, which Daniel also interprets, and which is focused on Nebuchadnezzar himself. Beginning with chapter 7, however, God initiates the remaining revelations to Daniel personally, each of which reveals various aspects of the future events which would be involved in the end of the old covenant and the establishment of the new covenant.

The dream-vision of Daniel 7 "in the first year of Belshazzar" (c. 553 BC) comes to Daniel fifty years after Nebuchadnezzar's dream of Daniel 2 "in the second year of the reign of Nebuchadnezzar" (c. 604 BC). It parallels chapter 2 and expands on the events involved in the establishment of the kingdom of God.

Daniel 7 may well be seen as the "high point" of the book in that it presents the heavenly enthronement of the Messiah, the Son of Man. It is also a pivotal section of the book, as it is the climax of the Aramaic section of Daniel, followed by the use of Hebrew for the remaining narrative.

It is also the point at which God's personal revelations to Daniel begin and a change of focus occurs. This change is suggested by the fact that chapter 7 also breaks the chronological sequence of events, as the vision of chapter 7 occurs during the Babylonian reign, while the preceding account of King Belshazzar's banquet of chapter 5 comes some fourteen years later when the Babylonians are suddenly overthrown by the Persians. Likewise, the account of Daniel and the den of lions in chapter 6 happens after the Persians have conquered them.

Furthermore, no longer will the content of Daniel be centered on God's relationship with Babylonian kings such as Nebuchadnezzar and Belshazzar, or Darius the Mede, and on the situation of Daniel and his friends while in exile. Now the focus shifts to the future of "the glorious land," the holy city of Jerusalem, the Jewish temple, and of God's people in general.

Four Great Beasts

Four beasts are seen coming out of the "great sea" (Dan. 7:2), which here (as explained to Daniel in verse 17), as elsewhere in Scripture, refers to the Gentile world of nations and peoples (see Isa. 17:12). Accordingly, all the beasts are ceremonially "unclean" animals of prey.

Here each animal represents a successive kingdom, each of which includes a succession of kings, and each of which also, in turn, will dominate God's people and control His holy place of Jerusalem and the site of the Jewish temple.

The four beasts equal the same four kingdoms as in Daniel 2:[1]

1. The winged lion was a well-known symbol of the Babylonian Empire. Having its wings torn off and being given "the heart of a man" suggests the experience of Nebuchadnezzar in chapter 4 that results in his being humbled before the Most High God.

2. The bear was a common image of the Medo-Persian Empire. The three ribs apparently represent their three major conquests of Lydia (modern Turkey), Egypt, and Babylon.

3. The leopard with four heads and four wings readily corresponds to Alexander the Great's rapid conquering of that area of the world and the establishment of the Greek Empire. When he died young, his empire was ultimately divided between four of his generals.

4. The terrifying beast with ten horns would then be the Roman Empire. It will "devour the whole earth" (7:23)—it will conquer the land of God's people and all the surrounding regions to which they had spread. This beast will appear again later, with features of the other three beasts, in the visions of Revelation 12–20 (Rev. 13:2). Exactly how it was different from all the former beasts is unexplained, perhaps because its leaders will deliberately attempt to kill the Messiah.

The Courtroom of Heaven and the Son of Man

Other than the brief clarification that the four beasts represent a sequence of four kingdoms, this vision quickly focuses on the fourth kingdom and on heavenly events which occur at that time, during the fourth kingdom. During the reign of the fourth-kingdom beast, the Roman Empire, the scene of a heavenly courtroom is introduced. The court is seated, books are opened, and judgment on the four kingdoms is dispensed.

Important questions arise at this point: What is meant by this judgment and when is it occurring? The key to answering these questions again is in understanding the spiritual realities behind these earthly kingdoms. In the finished work of Christ on the cross, He conquered these spiritual principalities and powers and their "right" to reign over the Gentile world and to accuse the saints before the throne of God (Job 1:6–12; Jude 9). This explains the phrasing of verse 12, that the previous beasts had been stripped of their (political) authority, but "their lives were prolonged for a season and a time," with their gods and goddesses continuing to have a measure of spiritual influence and power during the Roman period, until the finished work of Christ would be accomplished and all authority in heaven and on earth would be given to Him.

This judgment takes place prior to, or at the same time as, Jesus' ascension to heaven, as the courtroom scene is immediately followed by the enthronement of "one like a son of man" (Dan. 7:9–14) as King of kings, and His everlasting kingdom is established. While "son of man" is repeatedly used by God in reference to Ezekiel in His revelations to that prophet, there it simply means a human man. It is here in Daniel 7 that Jesus gets His favorite self-description as "Son of Man," as seen in His repeated verbal allusions to this passage, regarding His authority, power, and coming judgment.[2]

Ten Kings and an Eleventh King

The confusion comes in 7:19–25: Who are the ten "horns" (kings) and the additional "little horn" (king) who are being described as part of the Roman "beast" (vv. 8, 20–25)? The reference to another king who will subdue three kings (v. 24) makes it clear that the rule of these kings would be sequential rather than contemporaneous.

What eleven Roman rulers are being described? Or, as some have speculated, does this suddenly, at some point, somehow jump two thousand years into the future and a revived "Roman Empire" in our day? If not, are they Roman emperors? Or could they instead be the sequence of eleven rulers of Jerusalem and Judea under the Romans, between Jesus' death and the Jewish revolt in AD 66? This is unclear, and there is a rationale, though not without problems, for each of the following scenarios:

1. If they are Roman emperors and begin with Julius Caesar (as the Jewish historian Josephus does), followed by Octavian ("Augustus"), Tiberius, Gaius Caligula, Claudius, Nero, Galba, Otho, and Vitellius, then Vespasian would be the tenth and Titus would be the eleventh.[3]

2. If they begin with Augustus as the first official emperor, then Titus would be the tenth, and his brother, Domitian, who followed him, would be the eleventh.

3. If the focus is instead specifically on the rulers of Jerusalem, Judea, and the Jews, it could be seen to begin with Pontius Pilate as the ruler at Jesus' death and then end with Gessius Florus as the eleventh, who was ruler when the Jews revolted and instigated and to some extent encouraged the Jewish revolt.[4]

The other, and I believe most likely, solution, however, is to view this from a distinctively Jewish standpoint: the Roman control over God's people, the Jews, and God's place, Jerusalem, had begun with the Roman general Pompey conquering Jerusalem in 63 BC. At that point in time, the Roman rulers were a triumvirate of Julius Caesar, Pompey, and Crassus, who ruled the Roman world together. After Crassus and Pompey died, Julius Caesar became the sole Roman ruler. After Julius Caesar was assassinated, there was a second triumvirate of Mark Anthony, Lepidus, and Octavian. Of this threesome, Octavian eventually established sole control and later took the title of Emperor Augustus Caesar. The ten individual Roman rulers over the conquered Jews then (Dan. 7:24), *from their perspective*, would be Pompey, Julius, Augustus, Tiberius, Claudius, Gaius Caligula, and Nero as the first seven, followed by the three brief rules of Galba, Otho, and Vitellius during "the year of the four emperors," a time of chaos and civil war throughout the Roman Empire after Nero died with no son to succeed him as emperor. The eleventh ruler would be, then, Vespasian, who ended the Roman civil war, subdued the supporters of the three other claimants to the throne who had each briefly presumed to rule (Dan. 7:8, 20, 24), and established himself as the new emperor.[5] This perspective best fits verses 20 ("before which three of them fell") and 24 ("he shall put down three kings"). He was "different from the former ones" (v. 24) either in that he was not descended from the family line of the Caesars and began a new hereditary Roman dynasty, or perhaps in the severity of his attacks on God's people, as we will see below.

Vespasian as the Eleventh King

What do we know about Vespasian? Did he "speak words against the Most High ... wear out the saints ... think to change the times and the law" (Dan. 7:25)? Although the Jewish historian Josephus portrays Vespasian in a very positive light, it is because Vespasian was his benefactor and friend, not to mention being his emperor, whom he would not dare to criticize. To the Romans he was their hero who had saved the Roman Empire from the chaos after Nero's death. However, we know a number of things about Vespasian that can be seen to fit a more evil image from the perspective of God's people:

1. He was the Roman general who led the Roman army in a brutal crushing of the Jewish revolt throughout Galilee, as recounted by Josephus.[6]
2. After conquering Galilee, Vespasian left to become the Roman emperor, naming his son, Titus, as com-

mander of the army that would ultimately destroy Jerusalem and burn the Jewish temple, thus ending the temple sacrifices.

3. Then the annual pilgrimages to the temple in Jerusalem for the great festivals of the Jewish life were ended, with a Roman army encamped in Jerusalem to control the limited number of Jews allowed to still live there.

4. Under Vespasian's rule, the freedom of the Jews to rule over their own affairs through the Sanhedrin according to their own laws was also ended, as they would now be governed by a military representative of the emperor.[7]

5. According to Josephus, over a million Jews perished during the defense of Jerusalem. Afterward, nearly one hundred thousand Jews were sold as slaves. Recent archaeological evidence suggests that the proceeds from their sale and the plundered booty of the enormous wealth taken from the Jewish temple were used by Vespasian to finance the building of the gigantic Roman Coliseum.[8]

6. Vespasian also used the spoils of the war to build a theater in Antioch, where he had demolished a synagogue, as well as a concert hall in Caesarea, also on a former synagogue site.[9]

7. Furnishings from the temple—including the golden table for the "show bread," the seven-branched golden "menorah" lamp-stand, and the musical instruments used by the Levites—were deposited in a pagan temple of peace, which he built in Rome.[10]

8. Vespasian used the purple drapes from the Jewish temple in his own palace.[11]

9. Perhaps worst of all for the Jews, under Vespasian's rule they were even forced to support pagan worship. All Jews throughout the Roman Empire were forced by Vespasian to do something they had never been asked to do before by any Roman ruler: The half-shekel "temple tax" each Jewish adult male was required to give each year to support the temple in Jerusalem now was replaced with a two-denarius tax on all Jews, male and female, young and old, to be given to the pagan temple of Jupiter in Rome. (Of course, this would have impacted the Jewish followers of Jesus as well.)[12]

10. Finally, like King Herod at Jesus' birth, Vespasian even tried to find and kill the Messiah. The early Christian writer Hegessipus writes that after the conquest of Jerusalem Vespasian ordered that a search be made for all descendants of David so that no member of the royal house should be left among the Jews, which resulted in another great persecution.[13] Both Herod and Vespasian, the evil rulers over God's people at the beginning and at the end of "the time of the end," took the claims of a Jewish Messiah from David's line very seriously and, consequently, deliberately attempted to find and destroy Him.

Taking all of the acts of Vespasian against God's people together, we can see he was certainly someone who could appropriately be described as one who would "speak words against the Most High ... wear out the saints ... think to change the times and the law."

A Time, Times, and Half a Time

Daniel 7:25 further states that "the saints ... shall be given into his hand for a time, times, and half a time." This is commonly assumed to represent three and a half years. If so, this would be an apt approximation of the period of Vespasian's roles in subduing the Jewish revolt, from the invasion of the Roman army under him, in the spring of AD 67, to the destruction of the temple with him as Emperor, on August 7, AD 70, or the final end of any resistance in Jerusalem, on September 8, AD 70. During this period, God handed the rebellious Jews, Jerusalem, and the Jewish temple over to the Romans for destruction.

The Inheritance of the Saints

"But the court shall sit in judgment" (v. 26) refers back to the judgment envisioned in verse 10. Vespasian and the Roman army would be God's agents to bring God's covenant-ending judgment on the Jews, yet Vespasian himself, and the spiritual principalities and powers behind him, would also be judged by God and would be completely destroyed. While it is not clear when and how this judgment would take place, it is clear that with the establishment of the new covenant, the finished work of Christ, His ultimate enthronement in heaven, and the establishment of His eternal kingdom, the time for judging has arrived.

God's people, through the work of Christ, are "the saints of the Most High (who) shall receive the kingdom and possess the kingdom forever" (v. 18). The Lord *has* pronounced judgment in favor of His people ("judgment was given for the saints of the Most High," v. 22), and the time has already come when all authority has been given to King Jesus (v. 14; also cf. Matt. 28:18). In Christ, and through His indwelling Holy Spirit at work in us and through us, we are "already but not yet fully" partakers of His kingdom, as He exercises His will through us.

Chapter 3

DANIEL 8: VISIONS OF
THE TIME OF THE END

In the third year of the reign of King Belshazzar a vision appeared to me, Daniel, after that which appeared to me at the first. And I saw in the vision; and when I saw, I was in Susa the citadel, which is in the province of Elam. And I saw in the vision, and I was at the Ulai canal. I raised my eyes and saw, and behold, a ram standing on the bank of the canal. It had two horns, and both horns were high, but one was higher than the other, and the higher one came up last. I saw the ram charging westward and northward and southward. No beast could stand before him, and there was no one who could rescue from his power. He did as he pleased and became great.

As I was considering, behold, a male goat came from the west across the face of the whole earth, without touching the ground. And the goat had a conspicuous horn between his eyes. He came to the ram with the two horns, which I had seen standing on the bank of the canal, and he ran at him in his powerful wrath. I saw him come close to the ram, and he was enraged against him and struck the ram and broke his two horns. And the ram had no power to stand before him, but he cast him down to the ground and trampled on him. And there was no one who could rescue the ram from his power. Then the goat became exceedingly great, but when he was strong, the great horn was broken, and instead of it there came up four conspicuous horns toward the four winds of heaven.

Out of one of them came a little horn, which grew exceedingly great toward the south, toward the east, and toward the glorious land. It grew great, even to the host of heaven. And some of the host and some of the stars it threw down to the ground and trampled on them. It became great, even as great as the Prince of the host. And the regular burnt offering was taken away from him, and the place of his sanctuary was overthrown. And a host will be given over to it together with the regular burnt offering because of transgression, and it will throw truth to the ground, and it will act and prosper. Then I heard a holy one speaking, and another holy one said to the one who spoke, "For how long is the vision concerning the regular burnt offering, the transgression that makes desolate, and the giving over of the sanctuary and host to be trampled underfoot?" And he said to me, "For 2,300 evenings and mornings. Then the sanctuary shall be restored to its rightful state."

When I, Daniel, had seen the vision, I sought to understand it. And behold, there stood before me one having the appearance of a man. And I heard a man's voice between the banks of the Ulai, and it called, "Gabriel, make this man understand the vision." So he came near where I stood. And when he came, I was frightened and fell on my face. But he said to me, "Understand, O son of man, that the vision is for the time of the end."

And when he had spoken to me, I fell into a deep sleep with my face to the ground. But he touched me and made me stand up. He said, "Behold, I will make known to you what shall be at the latter end of the indignation, for it refers to the appointed time of the end. As for the ram that you saw with the two horns, these are the kings of Media and Persia. And the goat is the king of Greece. And the great horn between his eyes is the first king. As for the horn that was broken, in place of which four others arose, four kingdoms shall arise from his nation, but not with his power. And at the latter end of their kingdom, when the transgressors have reached their limit, a king of bold face, one who understands riddles, shall arise. His power shall be great—but not by his own power; and he shall cause fearful destruction and shall succeed in what he does, and destroy mighty men and the people who are the saints. By his cunning he shall make deceit prosper under his hand, and in his own mind he shall become great. Without warning he shall destroy many. And he shall even rise up against the Prince of princes, and he shall be broken—but by no human hand. The vision of the evenings and the mornings that has been told is true, but seal up the vision, for it refers to many days from now."

And I, Daniel, was overcome and lay sick for some days. Then I rose and went about the king's business, but I was appalled by the vision and did not understand it.

—Daniel 8:1–27

Overview

BEGINNING WITH DANIEL 8:1 the remainder of the text of Daniel was written in Hebrew again, emphasizing that the focus now narrows to events particularly related to the Jews.

This second vision to Daniel is given in the third year of Babylonian king Belshazzar's reign (about 551 BC), two years after the vision of the four beasts recounted in chapter 7.

In this vision the disputed texts are Daniel 8:9–14 and 8:17–25. They are both usually understood by scholars to refer to the Seleucid king Antiochus IV Epiphanes. In his efforts to "Hellenize" the Jews, Antiochus ordered a stop to temple sacrifices, removed the high priest, profaned the temple by bringing in an object dedicated to the god Zeus, sacrificed a pig on the altar, looted the temple, killed many Jews, forbade circumcision, compelled Jews to offer sacrifices to idols, banned the observance of Sabbaths and festivals, made possessing a copy of the Scriptures a capital offense, and referred to himself as "theos epiphanies"—"god manifest."[1]

For those scholars who don't accept the possibility of predictive prophecy and who see Daniel as having been written in the second century, the evils of Antiochus are the natural referents. This is likewise true for many Jewish commentators who reject Jesus as being the Messiah, and thus don't consider Daniel's prophecies as being related in any way to Him and the new covenant.

However, covenantally, an alternative interpretation seems more likely for each of these passages. The vision of Daniel 8 gives Daniel greater detail about "the time of the end" (of the old covenant), focusing first on the end of the old covenant, and then on the beginning events involved in establishing the new covenant. Specifically, it introduces the events at the end of that period, involving the Jewish rebellion against the Romans, which culminated in the destruction of the Jewish temple in AD 70, and it also portrays the establishment of Herod as king of the Jews under the Romans as the beginning point for this "time of the end."

A Ram and a Goat

The identities of the ram and the goat are revealed in verses 20–22. The ram was a traditional symbol of the king of Persia, who would carry a gold ram's head when leading his army.[2] The two horns represent the merger of the Persians with the Medes, with the Persians coming to dominate over time. The swiftly advancing and very aggressive goat with a prominent horn, coming from the west, symbolizes the rapid advance of the army of the Greeks under Alexander the Great. The Greeks conquered the Medo-Persian Empire, but at the height of Greek power, Alexander died suddenly at the age of thirty-three, in 323 BC.

Four Horns and Another Horn

Upon Alexander's death, his empire was eventually divided among his four regional commanders, resulting in four kingdoms of lesser power—one centered in Greece, one in Asia Minor, one in Egypt, and one in Syria and Babylon. Of these four kingdoms, the Ptolemy dynasty based in Egypt and the Seleucid dynasty in the area of Babylon and Syria, in the eastern remains of Alexander's empire, would become adversaries in a protracted, centuries-long battle for control of the Lord's people and their land, "the glorious land" of verse 9, as would be described in more detail in the vision of Daniel 11.

Verse 9 introduces "a little horn, which grew exceedingly great toward the south, toward the east, and toward the glorious land." Most commentators have assumed that this is a reference to the evil Antiochus IV "Epiphanes" of the Seleucid Empire. However, two factors suggest that this horn instead represents the Roman Empire. First, the growth toward the south, the east, and the glorious land fits the historic spread of the early Roman Empire, while this was not so true of Antiochus' reign. Also, unlike the "horns" of chapter 7, the four horns here represent not just individual kings, but four kingdoms that would develop from the remains of the Greek Empire, as is made clear in verse 22. The horn in 8:9 thus represents a *kingdom* (as with the other horns), not just one *king*, such as Antiochus. The new horn that grows "exceedingly great toward the south, toward the east, and toward the glorious land" (v. 9) "at the latter end of their kingdom" (v. 23) is then readily identifiable as the Roman Empire.

The Conquering Horn, Rebellion, and Temple Calamities

Following this understanding, verses 10–14 describe the rule of the Roman Empire over the Jewish people and their land, ultimately resulting in the Jewish rebellion in AD 66, and leading to the destruction of the Jewish temple and the end of the daily offering of the old covenant animal sacrifices.

The "host of heaven" (v. 10) is sometimes used in Scripture in reference to angelic armies or the stars, but also symbolizes the people of God, as in Genesis 12:3; 15:5; and Exodus 12:41. So, too, here in verses 10 and 12, and as reflected in 8:24–25 and 12:3.

The Jews and their religious system "were given over to" the Romans (v. 12) by the Lord, as He had earlier done using the Babylonian army (cf. 2 Kings 24:2; Hab.1:6). The Babylonians were both the agent of God's wrath and the subsequent object of God's wrath themselves, as the Lord had made clear to Habakkuk and other prophets. So, too, would it be with the Romans.

The question between two angelic beings in verse 13, which is answered for Daniel in verse 14, focuses on a specific part of the previous vision—the time period involving the end of the daily temple sacrifices, the transgression that results in the temple's desolation, and the giving over of the sanctuary and many of the people to be killed. This would happen during the time of the Roman Empire with the Jewish revolt of AD 66–70.

How much time would be involved for all of this to happen? The answer is "For 2,300 evenings and mornings. Then the sanctuary shall be restored to its rightful state" (v. 1). Though this could be taken to represent 2,300 days, the references to the daily sacrifices, which, according to the Law given through Moses in Exodus 29:38–42 (also Num. 28:3–8; and note Dan. 9:21) were required to be done each morning and evening, suggest it is more likely that this refers to 1,150 days, roughly three years and two months by the Jewish calendar. This would have been from the invasion of the Roman army in the spring of AD 67 to crush the Jewish "transgression that makes desolate," to the ending of the daily temple sacrifices in July of AD 70 and the "giving over of the sanctuary" for destruction.

The Hebrew word *sadaq*, translated in the ESV of verse 14 as "restored to its rightful state," is used forty times in the Old Testament, and is variously translated as "reconsecrated," "reconstituted," "cleansed," "made righteous," "vindicated," "justified," "declared innocent," or "properly restored." If what is in view in verses 13–14, then, is the climactic end of the old covenant period, the sense here is of the vindication of all the old covenant animal sacrifices with the establishment of the new covenant, based on the new and perfect, final, atoning sacrifice of Christ (cf. Heb. 9:11–26).

Gabriel and the Interpretation of the Vision

At this point the angel Gabriel appears to Daniel and is charged to explain the vision to Daniel. The presence of Gabriel would seem to be significant, particularly since Gabriel appears in the Old Testament only here in 8:16 and in 9:21. In each case his role is to inform Daniel regarding the events that would end the old covenant and establish the new. Gabriel is found again only in Luke 1, where he appears to Zechariah and Mary to announce the arrival of the Messiah to establish the new covenant. Gabriel was the one who was honored to be the herald of the change of covenants.

The Time of the End

Daniel is instructed that the vision concerns "the time of the end" (v.17). The end of the old covenant is in mind, not the end of the world. How so? This same phrase is found in 8:17, 19; 11:35, 40; and 12:4, 9. The references in Daniel 11 are particularly helpful in defining how we should understand this period. Daniel 11:35 suggests that it begins shortly after the terrors of Antiochus IV are finally challenged by the Jews, resulting in a brief period of independence under the Jewish Hasmonean kings. Daniel 11:40–41 indicates that Rome (which had conquered the Seleucids and is the new "king of the north") gains control of "the glorious land" "at the time of the end." Thus, the period of "the time of the end" envisioned in Daniel would seem to begin with the Roman conquest of "the glorious land" and the establishment of the rule of Herod over the Jews as "puppet king" under the Romans. Then the key political entities would be in place for the coming of the Messiah. This "time of the end" would climax with the destruction of the temple and the formal end of all the old covenant forms of relating to God that were associated with it.

An Evil King Opposed to God

We have seen that commentators have often been misled to understand the "little horn" of verse 9 as referring to Antiochus IV Epiphanes. Similarly, Antiochus is commonly understood to be the "king of bold face" of verses 23–25. But, again, there is a different answer that makes better sense of the vision and its covenantal significance. While Antiochus IV will be mentioned in the detailed historical chronology provided in the vision of chapter 11, his despicable acts have only a temporary and limited significance when compared to the role of Herod the Great and his descendants during the life of Christ. In one sense Herod the Great's crime was much worse than those of Antiochus. While Antiochus tried to forcibly Hellenize the Jews of his day, King Herod took seriously the prophecies of the coming Messiah King and sought to deny their fulfillment when he very intentionally tried to kill the baby Messiah (cf. Dan. 8:25; Matt. 2:16). After him, his son, Herod Antipas, would be complicit in the crucifixion of Christ.

Herod the Great

The description given in the text of Daniel 8:23–25 can readily be seen to fit Herod the Great.

- "And at the latter end of their kingdom" (the last days of the four parts of Alexander's Greek empire, v. 22)
- "when the transgressors have reached their limit, a king of bold face, one who understands riddles, shall arise." (Through deceit, ruthlessness, and political intrigue, Herod gained and maintained power, as extensively recounted by Josephus and others.)
- "His power shall be great—but not by his own power." (He was assisted in gaining power by the Romans.)
- "and he shall cause fearful destruction and shall succeed in what he does" (Herod was incredibly successful, as attested by his numerous grand

building projects and his long reign, despite his many actions that were hated by the Jews: He repeatedly changed high priests and locked up their vestments under his personal control; he plundered the tomb of King David; he introduced a law for theft contrary to Jewish law; he had nine wives; and he introduced the decadent Greek theater and games into Jerusalem.)

- "and destroy mighty men and the people who are the saints. By his cunning he shall make deceit prosper under his hand, and in his own mind he shall become great. Without warning he shall destroy many." (He killed his own sons, killed three hundred army officers, killed the remaining members of the Hasmonean family, removed and drowned the high priest, tortured and killed many opponents, killed a group of Pharisees who opposed him, burned alive forty men who tore down the Roman eagle when it was placed over the temple gate, and plotted to have all the leaders of the Jews killed upon his death so people would mourn at that time.)

- "And he shall even rise up against the Prince of princes" (He believed the magi and deliberately attempted to kill the Messiah when Jesus was a baby in Bethlehem.)

- "and he shall be broken—but by no human hand." (Herod died of a horrible internal disease involving terrible itching, severe intestinal pain, an inflamed abdomen, gangrene of his genitals, worms, asthma, and convulsions. Josephus explained this "rotting away from within" as God's punishment of him.)[3]

Summary

Thematically, the two-part vision of Daniel 8 expands the topic of the dreams of Daniel 2 and 7, by focusing on the transitional "time of the end" (of the old covenant and the establishment of the new covenant), with emphasis on the events at the very *end* of that period (the Jewish rebellion culminating in the destruction of the temple and the end of sacrifices) and the events at the very *beginning* of that period (the reign of Herod at the time of the birth of Christ).

Chapter 9

DANIEL 9: LOOKING BEYOND
A RESTORED JERUSALEM

In the first year of Darius the son of Ahasuerus, by descent a Mede, who was made king over the realm of the Chaldeans— in the first year of his reign, I, Daniel, perceived in the books the number of years that, according to the word of the LORD to Jeremiah the prophet, must pass before the end of the desolations of Jerusalem, namely, seventy years.

Then I turned my face to the Lord God, seeking him by prayer and pleas for mercy with fasting and sackcloth and ashes. I prayed to the LORD my God and made confession, saying, "O Lord, the great and awesome God, who keeps covenant and steadfast love with those who love him and keep his commandments, we have sinned and done wrong and acted wickedly and rebelled, turning aside from your commandments and rules. We have not listened to your servants the prophets, who spoke in your name to our kings, our princes, and our fathers, and to all the people of the land. To you, O Lord, belongs righteousness, but to us open shame, as at this day, to the men of Judah, to the inhabitants of Jerusalem, and to all Israel, those who are near and those who are far away, in all the lands to which you have driven them, because of the treachery that they have committed against you. To us, O LORD, belongs open shame, to our kings, to our princes, and to our fathers, because we have sinned against you. To the Lord our God belong mercy and forgiveness, for we have rebelled against him and have not obeyed the voice of the LORD our God by walking in his laws, which he set before us by his servants the prophets. All Israel has transgressed your law and turned aside, refusing to obey your voice. And the curse and oath that are written in the Law of Moses the servant of God have been poured out upon us, because we have sinned against him. He has confirmed his words, which he spoke against us and against our rulers who ruled us, by bringing upon us a great calamity. For under the whole heaven there has not been done anything like what has been done against Jerusalem. As it is written in the Law of Moses, all this calamity has come upon us; yet we have not entreated the favor of the LORD our God, turning from our iniquities and gaining insight by your truth. Therefore the LORD has kept ready the calamity and has brought it upon us, for the LORD our God is righteous in all the works that he has done, and we have not obeyed his voice. And now, O Lord our God, who brought your people out of the land of Egypt with a mighty hand, and have made a name for yourself, as at this day, we have sinned, we have done wickedly.

"O Lord, according to all your righteous acts, let your anger and your wrath turn away from your city Jerusalem, your holy hill, because for our sins, and for the iniquities of our fathers, Jerusalem and your people have become a byword among all who are around us. Now therefore, O our God, listen to the prayer of your servant and to his pleas for mercy, and for your own sake, O Lord, make your face to shine upon your sanctuary, which is desolate. O my God, incline your ear and hear. Open your eyes and see our desolations, and the city that is called by your name. For we do not present our pleas before you because of our righteousness, but because of your great mercy. O Lord, hear; O Lord, forgive. O Lord, pay attention and act. Delay not, for your own sake, O my God, because your city and your people are called by your name."

While I was speaking and praying, confessing my sin and the sin of my people Israel, and presenting my plea before the LORD my God for the holy hill of my God, while I was speaking in prayer, the man Gabriel, whom I had seen in the vision at the first, came to me in swift flight at the time of the evening sacrifice. He made me understand, speaking with me and saying, "O Daniel, I have now come out to give you insight and understanding. At the beginning of your pleas for mercy a word went out, and I have come to tell it to you, for you are greatly loved. Therefore consider the word and understand the vision.

"Seventy weeks are decreed about your people and your holy city, to finish the transgression, to put an end to sin, and to atone for iniquity, to bring in everlasting righteousness, to seal both vision and prophet, and to anoint a most holy place. Know therefore and understand that from the going out of the word to restore and build Jerusalem to the coming of an anointed one, a prince, there shall be seven weeks. Then for sixty-two weeks it shall be built again with squares and moat, but in a troubled time. And after the sixty-two weeks, an anointed one shall be cut off and shall have nothing. And the people of the prince who is to come shall destroy the city and the sanctuary. Its end shall come with a flood, and to the end there shall be war. Desolations are decreed. And he shall make a strong covenant with many for one week, and for half of the week he shall put an end to sacrifice and offering. And on the wing of abominations shall come one who makes desolate, until the decreed end is poured out on the desolator."

—Daniel 9:1–27

Daniel's Prayer

WHEN THE BABYLONIANS are conquered by the Medes and the Persians, Daniel is reminded of the word of the Lord that had been given to the prophet Jeremiah, that the desolation of Jerusalem would last seventy years. In 605 BC, as Nebuchadnezzar came to power as king of Babylon, Jeremiah had prophesied that the Lord would allow him to conquer the people of Judah, make their land a desolate wasteland, and force them to serve him for seventy years (Jer. 25:1–11). Daniel, himself, was among those taken to Babylon in 605 BC (Dan. 1:1–6). At the end of that seventy years the Babylonians would themselves be punished, and the Jewish exiles in Babylon would be allowed to return to their land (Jer. 29:1–10).

It is reasonable to think that Daniel would also have known of the prophecies that had been given through Isaiah of a man named Cyrus, who would be used by the Lord to judge the Babylonians, free the exiles, and decree and enable the rebuilding of Jerusalem and the temple (Isa. 44:28–45:13). Now that the Babylonians have been conquered and Cyrus the Persian is on the throne, Daniel prays on behalf of his people, Jerusalem, and the temple sanctuary, that the Lord would be faithful to His prophetic promises.

This seventy-year period of desolation and exile was fulfilled in two senses. Focusing on the desolation of the land, the time of the Babylonian domination lasted from the initial Babylonian conquest of Judah in 605 BC until the exiles were able to return and reestablish themselves in the land following the decree of Cyrus in 539 BC. In addition, in light of the context and its emphasis on the desolation of the city and the temple, an alternative period would be, as Ezra recounts, from the temple's destruction by the Babylonians in 586 BC until it was rebuilt and rededicated in 516 BC.

Gabriel and the Lord's Response

In response to Daniel's prayer on behalf of his people, Gabriel again comes to Daniel to give him "insight and understanding" (Dan. 9:22). The vision he subsequently reveals goes far beyond a confirmation that the seventy-year exile would end, that the land would again be inhabited, and that Jerusalem and the temple would be rebuilt. Rather, Gabriel's message focuses on the coming of the Messiah, the Anointed One, and the revelation of a further desolation at the end of the old covenant age. As in the vision of chapter 8, Gabriel again is herald of key events involved in the establishment of the new covenant and the end of the old covenant.

Six Aspects of the Work of Christ

While there is some ambiguity about the specific understanding of what is meant by each phrase of verse 24, the six phrases can best be understood in regard to the fullness of the atoning work of Christ through His suffering and death on the cross, His subsequent resurrection, ascension, and enthronement, and in His judgment (through the Roman army, which He used as "his troops," as in Matt. 22:7) on Jerusalem, the temple, and the Jews of that generation, which ended the old covenant era.

The first three phrases involve the work of Christ in dealing with sin and transgression:

"To finish the transgression" is readily related to God's judgment on the wicked Jews of Jesus' generation for their culmination of evil in rejecting Him. (See, for example, Matt. 21:33ff; 23:32, 35–39; 1 Thess. 2:15–16)

"To put an end to sin" clearly speaks more broadly of the atoning death of Christ on the cross as a sacrifice for sin, as in John 1:29 and Hebrews 1:3; 9:26–28; and 10:12.

Likewise, His self-sacrifice "to atone for iniquity" is also referenced in Romans 3:25; Colossians 1:20–22; and Hebrews 2:17.

The latter three phrases can be seen to deal with the establishment of the new covenant:

"To bring in everlasting righteousness" points to the standing we enjoy of being declared righteous in Christ, as expressed in passages such as Romans 3:20–22 and 10:2–4.

"To seal both vision and prophet" can be seen to include both Jesus' claim "to fulfill all that is written" (Luke 21:22), as well as the ending of visions and prophecy as authoritative Scripture, once the New Testament writings as the authoritative Word of God presenting the new covenant had been finished.

"To anoint a most holy place" can actually mean the "Most Holy One" or the "Most Holy Place," and literally could be translated "to anoint the Holiest of Holy Places." So, it can refer to Jesus, Himself, as "the Anointed One," as in Luke 4:18; to the heavenly temple, as in Hebrews 9:23–24; to the anointing by the Holy Spirit who indwells new covenant believers, as in 2 Corinthians 1:21; or all of the above!

Interpreting the Seventy "Weeks"

The starting and ending points for the seventy "weeks," in which these six things will be accomplished, have been much debated and variously interpreted. Which decree begins the seventy weeks? What event ends the sixty-nine weeks? Who is the "anointed one"? What "prince who is to come shall destroy the city and the sanctuary"? Is the seventieth week or any part of it (particularly the events of 9:27) now past or still future for us?

The Decree

The period being described begins with a decree to restore and rebuild Jerusalem. The most natural decree being referenced would be the decree of Cyrus in 538 BC, mentioned in 2 Chronicles 36:22–23 and Ezra 1:1–4.[1] This God-ordained use of Cyrus to rebuild Jerusalem and the Jewish temple is also expressed in Isaiah 44:27 and 45:13, and is further noted by the Jewish historian Josephus.[2]

There is an apparent problem with this conclusion, however. Assuming the seven weeks and the sixty-two weeks should be understood as years (totaling 69 x 7 years, or 483 years) and assuming the commonly accepted date for this decree as having been proclaimed in 538 BC, to use this decree as the starting point for the 483 years would seem to fall well short of the time of the ministry of Christ. This has led some to suggest an alternative starting point of one of the other edicts mentioned in Scripture—that of Darius (Ezra 5:3–7), of Artaxerxes I to Ezra (Ezra 7:11–26), or of Artaxerxes to Nehemiah (Neh. 2:1–8).

The best solution to this problem seems to lie in appreciating the limited and conflicting data upon which the chronology of the reigns of the Persian kings have been understood. The commonly assumed dating for the later kings of the Persian Empire is tenuous, based essentially on only one source, the Egyptian writer Ptolemy's "Canon of Kings" of the second century AD. But Ptolemy may have failed to properly consider co-regencies and overlapping reigns when deriving his commonly-assumed datings, and the eclipse data assumed to confirm the list is quite possibly unreliable, as well.[3] Also, evidence from other ancient writers suggests that the latter part of the Persian period has possibly been exaggerated by a confusion of names with titles or throne names, which has led to counting some kings twice.[4] Thus, by Ptolemy's list, the Persian Empire lasted 205 years, a revised chronology yields 123 years, while "the Jews also allotted only 52 years to the Persian period of their history"![5] Consequently, one cannot be too precise in determining the chronology of this period based on secular records alone, and the decree of Cyrus still seems the best option.

Until the Anointed One Comes

A total of sixty-nine "sevens" would pass between the decree and the coming of "an anointed one, a prince." Since the titles of "Messiah" and "Christ" have "an anointed one" as their root meaning, this seems to be a clear reference to the coming of Christ. Some have taken this end point to refer to the time of Jesus' baptism at the beginning of His earthly ministry, when He was about thirty years of age (Luke 3:23). Others, following the understanding of the early church historian Eusebius, see the time of the birth of Jesus, Messiah and Prince, announced by angels and heavenly signs, as "synchronizing with the fulfillment of the seven and sixty-two weeks of Daniel's prophecy."[6]

This latter view, of Jesus' birth being the end point of the sixty-nine sevens, would seem to also gain credence from the common Jewish expectation, presumably based on Daniel in significant part, of the imminent coming of the Messiah during the period around the time of Jesus' birth.[7] The Herodian faction of the Jews purportedly even suggested that Herod the Great was the Messiah, while the "Magi from the east" of Matthew 2 may well have known of the time frame given in Daniel's writings as impetus for their seeking of the newly born King of the Jews then.

The Initial Sixty-Nine Weeks

The ESV translators note an alternative translation for Daniel 9:25: "… there shall be seven weeks and sixty-two weeks. It shall be built again …," which seems to make better sense of the passage. The initial seven weeks of verse 25, assumed to be a period of forty-nine years, would be a time during which Jerusalem would be rebuilt, and reflects the resettlement of the city by the returning exiles, and the rebuilding of the temple. The books of Ezra and Nehemiah suggest the kinds of troubles encountered during this "troubled time." This period would be followed by a longer period. One that will be outlined in more detail in the next prophecy Daniel will receive (Dan. 11).

Seventy Weeks

There is a common Hebrew literary form, a chiastic structure (ABC-D-CBA), found in the account of the events recorded in "know therefore and understand that ..." (vv. 25–27). This chiasm is centered on the main point: "Its end shall come with a flood." In this case, the same themes and the same sequence of events between two decrees are re-expressed in parallel language on either side of it.

(A) A *decree* is issued to restore and rebuild Jerusalem (and resume the temple sacrifices).

(B) *The Anointed One* will be cut off, not for himself.

(C) The people of the coming ruler will *destroy* the city and the sanctuary.

(D) The end will come like a flood.

(C) There will be war until the end and *desolations*.

(B) He (*the Anointed One*) will make a covenant and put an end to sacrifice and offering.

(A) The *decreed* end of the temple (and the destruction of the city) will come.

Beyond pointing to the central theme—the end of the old covenant era—this inter-connected structure would also seem to make it wrong to suggest, as has been done by some, that verse 27 suddenly jumps two thousand years to events that still haven't happened.

Daniel 9:25–27 has been interpreted in many ways. It seems best to understand the end of the sixty-ninth week and the events of the seventieth week in regard to the key points of God's activity in establishing the new covenant in Jesus: the incarnation, Jesus' earthly ministry as Savior, and His ministry from heaven as Judge of the generation that would end the old covenant.

The "Anointed One" is Jesus. The first sixty-nine weeks end with the birth of Jesus, the Messiah and Prince, announced by angels and heavenly signs. Then there is a gap until the beginning of Jesus' public ministry and the seventieth week begins. The seventieth week focuses on establishing the new covenant and happens in two phases: first, the period of Jesus' public ministry, commonly understood to have been about three and a half years in length, climaxing in His death, resurrection, and ascension, inaugurating the new covenant; and later, another three and a half years of Jesus' ministry of judgment, expressed in the horrors of the period of the Jewish revolt from AD 66 to 70, which culminated in the destruction of the temple in AD 70, bringing the formal end to the old covenant era.[8]

Here is an annotated rendering of verses 26–27a:

And after the sixty-two weeks, an anointed one shall be cut off [Jesus will be crucified] and shall have nothing [or perhaps "but not for himself"]. And the people of the prince who is to come shall destroy the city and the sanctuary. [The Romans, who had been introduced in each of the previous visions, destroyed the temple and

Jerusalem in AD 70, acting as agents of judgment by King Jesus, as with God's use of the Babylonians previously.] Its end [the end of the old covenant] shall come with a flood, and to the end there shall be war. Desolations are decreed. And he [the Anointed One/Messiah] shall make a strong covenant with many for one week [The full work of Christ establishing the new covenant was comprised of two parts: first, bringing the fullness of salvation through His earthly ministry and death; and then, bringing judgment and desolation in AD 66–70,], and for half of the week he shall put an end to sacrifice and offering. [After His three and a half years of public ministry, He will die on the cross as the ultimate "Lamb of God who takes away the sin of the world" (John 1:29), replacing the repeated animal sacrifices and offerings of the old covenant.]

Abominations that Cause Desolation

The last part of verse 27 is unusually difficult to precisely translate with any certainty, and is arguably one of the most difficult texts in the entire Bible. The New International Version (NIV) translators, for example, give an alternative translation that would significantly alter the interpretation of it. A comparison with a few other translations, such as the excerpts below from the NIV, King James, and New King James translations, confirms the translational difficulties.

And at the temple he will set up an abomination that causes desolation, until the end that is decreed is poured out on him. (NIV)

And one who causes desolation will come upon the wing of the abominable temple, until the end that is decreed is poured out on the desolated city. (alternate NIV rendering)

And on the wing of abominations shall be one who makes desolate, even until the consummation, which is determined, is poured out on the desolate. (NKJV)

And for the overspreading of abominations he shall make it desolate, even until the consummation, and that determined shall be poured upon the desolate. (KJV and KJ21)

And on the wing of abominations shall come one who makes desolate, until the decreed end is poured out on the desolator. (ESV)

Assuming that the text is describing the events involved with the Jewish revolt of AD 66 and the ultimate destruction of the temple in AD 70, which Jesus had predicted, a rendering of this phrasing similar to the KJV wording would seem warranted: "And for the overspreading of abominations [cf. Matt. 23:32–38; 24:15; Luke 19:41–44] he [Jesus] shall make it [the temple] desolate, even until the consummation [of the old covenant era], and that determined shall be poured upon the desolate [the temple]."

As the Lord made clear through Ezekiel (Ezek. 24:21) regarding the Babylonian destruction of the city and burning of the temple, it is God Himself who allows the desecration of His temple and its destruction. How much more so once the new covenant in Jesus had made the temple sacrifices and rituals obsolete (see Heb. 8:13)!

Chapter 5

DANIEL 10-12: WAR UNTIL
THE "TIME OF THE END"

ANIEL 10 IS an introduction to Daniel 11–12 and offers a glimpse of the spiritual realities "behind the scenes" of historical events. The vision is given to him in response to the fact that Daniel was seeking to understand something (Dan. 10:12), apparently his desire to better understand the revelations of future events that he had already received. For Daniel, this latest vision— particularly the deliverance, resurrection, and spread of righteousness mentioned in 12:1–3—must have provided a significant measure of comfort after the previous accounts of evil people, abominations, the desolation of the temple, and the future trials of his people.

The details of the prophetic vision begin in 11:2. Daniel 11:2–35 has had a scholarly consensus concerning its general interpretation, based on the accounts of this period by ancient writers such as Livy, in Plutarch's *Life of Marc Antony*, and in 1 and 2 Maccabees.[1] The "king of the south" and "king of the north" throughout this narrative are a succession of individual kings of the Seleucid and Ptolemy dynasties, based in Syria and Egypt, respectively. Again, in the center, at the crossroads of this ongoing battle of dynasties, is "the glorious land" of the Jews.

The text of Daniel 11:2–35, with explanatory notes that reflect the extra-biblical historical record of the events of this period, follows:

Verse 2: And now I will show you the truth. Behold, three more kings shall arise in Persia [Cambyses, Smerdis Gaumata, and Darius I], and a fourth [Xerxes I] shall be far richer than all of them. And when he has become strong through his riches, he shall stir up all against the kingdom of Greece. [Xerxes I tried to conquer Greece, eventually leading the Greeks to unity under Alexander about one hundred years later.]

Verse 3: Then a mighty king shall arise, who shall rule with great dominion and do as he wills [Alexander the Great].

Verse 4: And as soon as he has arisen, his kingdom shall be broken and divided toward the four winds of heaven, but not to his posterity, nor according to the authority with which he ruled, for his kingdom shall be plucked up and go to others besides these. [As previously mentioned in Dan. 7:6; 8:8; and 22; with Cassander over Greece, Ptolemy over Egypt, Seleucus over Babylon, and Antigonus over Turkey and Syria originally.]

Verse 5: Then the king of the south [Ptolemy I] shall be strong, but one of his princes shall be stronger than he and shall rule, and his authority shall be a great authority

[Seleucus I, who had sought refuge with Ptolemy when attacked by Antigonus, had become a leader of Ptolemy's army].

Verse 6: After some years they shall make an alliance, and the daughter [Berenice] of the king of the south [Ptolemy II] shall come to the king of the north [Antiochus II] to make an agreement. But she shall not retain the strength of her arm, and he and his arm shall not endure, but she shall be given up, and her attendants, he who fathered her, and he who supported her in those times. [Antiochus's former wife, Laodice, conspired to have Bernice and Antiochus poisoned, and her father Ptolemy died at about the same time.]

Verse 7: And from a branch from her roots one shall arise in his place [Berenice's brother Ptolemy III]. He shall come against the army and enter the fortress of the king of the north [Seleucus II, and either Antioch or its port city, Seleucia], and he shall deal with them and shall prevail.

Verse 8: He shall also carry off to Egypt their gods with their metal images and their precious vessels of silver and gold, and for some years he shall refrain from attacking the king of the north. [There was more than two years of peace.]

Verse 9: Then the latter [Seleucus II] shall come into the realm of the king of the south but shall return to his own land.

Verse 10: His sons [Seleucus III and Antiochus III] shall wage war and assemble a multitude of great forces [62,000 soldiers, 6,000 cavalry, 102 elephants], which shall keep coming and overflow and pass through, and again shall carry the war as far as his fortress [Ptolemy's fortress at Raphia in southern Palestine].

Verse 11: Then the king of the south [Ptolemy IV], moved with rage, shall come out and fight against the king of the north [Antiochus III]. And he shall raise a great multitude, but it shall be given into his hand. [He was defeated at Raphia in 217 BC.]

Verses 12–13: And when the multitude is taken away, his heart shall be exalted, and he shall cast down tens of thousands, but he shall not prevail. [Antiochus lost nearly 10,000 soldiers in his victory at Raphia.] For the king of the north shall again raise a multitude, greater than the first. And after some years he shall come on with a great army and abundant supplies.

Verse 14: In those times many shall rise against the king of the south [After Ptolemy IV died, his six-year-old son, Ptolemy V, reigned during a time of insurrection.], and the violent among your own people shall lift themselves up [Jews who joined the forces of Antiochus] in order to fulfill the vision, but they shall fail. [The army of Ptolemy crushed the rebellion in 200 BC; the Jews had rebelled against the southern kingdom, only to later be conquered by the king of the north.]

Verse 15: Then the king of the north shall come and throw up siege-works and take a well-fortified city [Sidon]. And the forces of the south shall not stand, or even his best troops, for there shall be no strength to stand.

Verse 16: But he who comes against him [Antiochus] shall do as he wills, and none shall stand before him. And he shall stand in the glorious land, with destruction in his hand.

Verse 17: He shall set his face to come with the strength of his whole kingdom, and he shall bring terms of an agreement and perform them. He shall give him the daughter of women [Antiochus III gave his daughter Cleopatra I in marriage to Ptolemy V] to destroy the kingdom, but it shall not stand or be to his advantage. [Cleopatra aided her husband instead.]

Verse 18: Afterward he shall turn his face to the coastlands [Asia Minor and the Greek islands] and shall capture many of them, but a commander shall put an end to his insolence. Indeed, he shall turn his insolence back upon him. [Roman consul Scipio defeated Antiochus III at Magnesia in 190 BC, bringing Syria under nominal Roman control; Antiochus's son was taken to Rome as a prisoner.]

Verse 19: Then he shall turn his face back toward the fortresses of his own land, but he shall stumble and fall, and shall not be found. [Antiochus died in 187 BC.]

Verse 20: Then shall arise in his place [his son, Seleucus IV] one who shall send an exactor of tribute [Seleucus' finance minister, Heliodorus] for the glory of the kingdom. But within a few days he shall be broken, neither in anger nor in battle. [Seleucus IV was murdered in a conspiracy led by Heliodorus.]

Verse 21: In his place shall arise a contemptible person [Seleucus' younger brother, Antiochus IV, who took the title "Epiphanes," meaning "god-manifest"] to whom royal majesty has not been given. [He seized power while Seleucus' son was very young.] He shall come in without warning and obtain the kingdom [Syria/Palestine] by flatteries.

Verse 22: Armies shall be utterly swept away before him and broken [a summary statement of his military victories over Ptolemy], even the prince of the covenant. [He deposed and killed the high priest—the first time a ruler would interfere with the Jewish religious realm in this way.]

Verses 23–24: And from the time that an alliance is made with him he [Antiochus] shall act deceitfully, and he shall become strong with a small people. [He took the throne from his young nephew.] Without warning he shall come into the richest parts of the province, and he shall do what neither his fathers nor his fathers' fathers have done, scattering among them plunder, spoil, and goods. He shall devise plans against strongholds, but only for a time.

Verse 25: And he shall stir up his power and his heart against the king of the south [Ptolemy VI] with a great army. And the king of the south shall wage war with an exceedingly great and mighty army, but he shall not stand, for plots shall be devised against him. [His brother would declare himself king.]

Verse 26: Even those who eat his food shall break him. [Ptolemy's advisors gave him bad advice.] His army shall be swept away, and many shall fall down slain.

Verse 27: And as for the two kings [Antiochus IV and Ptolemy VI], their hearts shall be bent on doing evil. They shall speak lies at the same table, but to no avail, for the end is yet to be at the time appointed.

Verse 28: And he [Antiochus] shall return to his land with great wealth, but his heart shall be set against the holy covenant. And he shall work his will and return to his own land. [In 169 BC, Antiochus looted the treasury in the Jewish temple, built a military fort beside it, took the sacred vessels, and killed many Jews in the city.]

Verses 29–30: At the time appointed he shall return and come into the south, but it shall not be this time as it was before. For ships of Kittim [a Roman navy] shall come against him, and he shall be afraid and withdraw [he was humiliated by the Roman consul and forced to retreat], and shall turn back and be enraged and take action against the holy covenant. [He massacred many Jews and sold others as slaves; he made a law that possessing the Scriptures was punishable by death; he forbade circumcision, any sacrifices, or observing the Sabbath and feasts; and he forced Jews to eat pig meat and to sacrifice at idolatrous altars set up in various places.] He shall turn back and pay attention to those who forsake the holy covenant [those Jews who renounced their faith].

Verse 31: Forces from him shall appear and profane the temple and fortress, and shall take away the regular burnt offering. And they shall set up the abomination that makes desolate. [In 167 BC, after stopping the daily sacrifices, Antiochus built an altar in the Jewish temple to the pagan god Zeus, on which he had a pig slaughtered.]

Verse 32: He shall seduce with flattery those who violate the covenant, but the people who know their God shall stand firm and take action. [The Maccabeus family led a Jewish resistance that ultimately brought a period of independence.]

Verses 33–35: And the wise among the people shall make many understand [the godly leaders of the Jewish resistance movement—the Hasidim or "pious ones"], though for some days they shall stumble by sword and flame, by captivity and plunder. When they stumble, they shall receive a little help. And many shall join themselves to them with flattery, and some of the wise shall stumble, so that they may be refined, purified, and made white, until the time of the end, for it still awaits the appointed time. [After the Jewish revolt against Antiochus IV Epiphanes came a period (described in the Jewish literature known as 1 and 2 Maccabees, and in Josephus' *History of the Jews*) of continued fighting for independence from the Syrians, as well as infighting and civil war among the Jews. Civil, military, and religious leadership was combined under the high priest's leadership through much of this period, and was dominated by the Maccabeus/Hasmonean family and a priestly aristocracy. Then, in 63 BC the Romans under Pompey besieged and conquered Jerusalem. Eventually, the man known as Herod the Great was officially appointed by the Roman senate as king of Judea in 40 BC.]

A Tale of Two Witnesses

The four visions given to Daniel (beyond the interpretation of the dream of King Nebuchadnezzar in Daniel 2) come to him in pairs, with that of chapter 7 in 553 BC followed in 551 BC with that of chapter 8. The vision introduced in chapter 10, given in 536 BC, is likewise following relatively soon after the vision he received in 539 BC of the "seventy weeks" of years (Dan. 9). This pairing suggests an answer to the question of why the vision of Daniel 11:2–12:13 includes such a great amount of historical detail, which, for the liberal critic who discounts such prophetic specificity, is beyond belief. Even for someone who believes God is able to declare the future and then bring it to pass, the reason for all of the seemingly "irrelevant" details can seem hard to comprehend.

The answer is that the vision of Daniel 9 and that of Daniel 11–12 should be seen as two witnesses. In the law of Moses, "every charge may be established by the evidence of two or three witnesses" (Deut. 19:15; Matt. 18:16; John 8:17). Likewise, in biblical symbolism, doubling has the sense of establishing things with certainty (Jesus' teachings in John's Gospel are often begun with a double affirmation of "verily, verily" or "truly, truly," which is sometimes translated as, "I tell you the truth." Similarly Joseph's dual dreams are evidence of certainty, as noted in Gen.41:32.) Accordingly, these two visions point in complementary ways with prophetic certainty to the time of the coming of the Christ, the end of the old covenant, and the establishment of the new covenant. First, the vision of seventy weeks of years in Daniel 9 provides a precise overall time frame for when these events would take place. Then, the highly detailed vision of Daniel 11–12 confirms this by citing the extended sequence of historical events that would be played out during this same period.

The "King"

The section of this vision in dispute begins with Daniel 11:36. At this point in the text, commentators are confused as to the identity of the "king" now being introduced, who is not identified as either a "king of the north" or a "king of the south." Many assume this must be a continued reference to Antiochus IV Epiphanes, though the following events don't fit with the historical events of his life as we know them. This fact leads many other commentators to presume the narrative now shifts to some "Antichrist" king and events in an "end times" still in the future. However, the text is generally quite understandable simply as a continuation of the sequence of historical events leading up to Christ and focusing now on King Herod the Great and the rise of Roman dominance over the Beautiful Land. This is particularly so if "the king" now being introduced is a reference back to Herod as the king, who had earlier been described to Daniel in Daniel 8:19–25. For Daniel, that king, likewise coming on the scene at "the time of the end" (Dan. 8:19 and 11:35), would have been the most logical reference to such a king from his previous visions.

Daniel 11:36–39 summarizes Herod's life and character, while verses 40–45 recount the rise of Rome in relation to Herod and the Jews, culminating in his reign under the Romans as king of the Jews. This brings the narrative of the vision of Daniel 11–12 to the time of the birth of Christ and coincides with the same point in history as in the previous revelations—to the time of the fourth kingdom of Daniel 2 and the fourth/terrifying beast of Daniel 7, to the beginning of the "time of the end" of Daniel 8, and to the end of the sixty-nine weeks of Daniel 9.

And the king shall do as he wills. He shall exalt himself and magnify himself above every god, and shall speak astonishing things against the God of gods. He shall prosper till the indignation is accomplished; for what is decreed shall be done. He shall pay no attention to the gods of his fathers, or to the one beloved by women. He shall not pay attention to any other god, for he shall magnify himself above all. He shall honor the god of fortresses instead of these. A god whom his fathers did not know he shall honor with gold and silver, with precious stones and costly gifts. He shall deal with the strongest fortresses with the help of a foreign god. Those who acknowledge him he shall load with honor. He shall make them rulers over many and shall divide the land for a price.

At the time of the end, the king of the south shall attack him, but the king of the north shall rush upon him like a whirlwind, with chariots and horsemen, and with many ships. And he shall come into countries and shall overflow and pass through. He shall come into the glorious land. And tens of thousands shall fall, but these shall be delivered out of his hand: Edom and Moab and the main part of the Ammonites. He shall stretch out his hand against the countries, and the land of Egypt shall not escape. He shall become ruler of the treasures of gold and of silver, and all the precious things of Egypt, and the Libyans and the Cushites shall follow in his train. But news from the east and the north shall alarm him, and he shall go out with great fury to destroy and devote many to destruction. And he shall pitch his palatial tents between the sea and the glorious holy mountain. Yet he shall come to his end, with none to help him.

—Daniel 11:36–45

Herod the Great

The following notes reflect how this passage can be seen in regard to Herod the Great and his family line:

Verse 36: And the king [Herod the Great, installed by the Romans as "king of the Jews," as in Matt. 2:1 and Luke 1:5] shall do as he wills. He shall exalt himself and magnify himself above every god, and shall speak astonishing things against the God of gods [such as his decree to kill the Messiah as a baby in Bethlehem]. He [and his descendants] shall prosper till the indignation is accomplished [the Jewish revolt and Roman destruction of Jerusalem in AD 66–70]; for what is decreed shall be done.

Verse 37: He shall pay no attention to the gods of his fathers [Though king of the Jews, Herod was racially an Edomite/Idumean. His mother was apparently a Nabataean Arab; one legend is that his grandfather had served in the temple of Apollo. Herod also participated in worship of the Roman emperor], or to the one beloved by women. [It was the hope of every Jewish woman that she would be the mother of the Christ child; Herod tried to kill him.] He shall not pay attention to any other god, for he shall magnify himself above all.

Verse 38: He shall honor the god of fortresses instead of these. [Herod built the Antonia Fortress in Jerusalem overlooking the temple, as well as other palace fortresses at Masada, Herodium, and Jericho.] A god whom his fathers did not know he shall honor with gold and silver, with precious stones and costly gifts. [Participating in worship of the emperor Caesar, Herod sent great quantities of these valuables to his Roman overlords; he built a seaport city and named it Caesarea, renamed another city as Caesarea Philippi, sponsored sports events in honor of Caesar, rebuilt Samaria and named it Sebaste/Augustus, and named the

Antonia Fortress after Mark Antony. He placed a huge golden eagle, the symbol of imperial Rome, at the entrance to the temple. Josephus says about Herod, "there was not any place in his kingdom … that was permitted to be without somewhat that was for Caesar's honor; and when he had filled his own country with temples, he poured out like plentiful marks of his esteem into his provinces, and built many cities which he called Caesareas."][2]

Verse 39: He shall deal with the strongest fortresses with the help of a foreign god. [With Roman help, Herod gained control of Jerusalem after a three-month siege; Herod then built the fortress Tower of Antonia overlooking the temple, to keep control of activities in the area of the Temple.] Those who acknowledge him he shall load with honor. He shall make them rulers over many and shall divide the land for a price. [Herod was known to parcel out land that he wanted to control in case of emergency to people who supported him.]

Verse 40: At the time of the end, the king of the south [Cleopatra, the queen of Egypt, aided by Mark Antony] shall attack him [the beginning of the Actium War], but the king of the north [Now the Romans under Octavian, "Augustus," of Rome had conquered the Seleucids and he had become the new "king of the north."] shall rush upon him like a whirlwind, with chariots and horsemen, and with many ships. [Augustus' navy won a great victory at Actium, followed by an invasion with cavalry and chariots; significantly, there is no mention in the text of infantry, perhaps because Antony's infantry deserted him after the defeat at Actium.] And he shall come into countries and shall overflow and pass through. [Augustus would invade many countries and sweep through them like a flood, conquering North Africa, Egypt, Europe, modern Turkey and Syria, and Babylonia.]

Verse 41: He shall come into the glorious land. And tens of thousands shall fall, but these shall be delivered out of his hand: Edom and Moab and the main part of the Ammonites. [Note that these ethnic groups don't exist today. A Roman military expedition into this rugged area was defeated, so these peoples were able to maintain a measure of independence from Rome.]

Verses 42–43: He shall stretch out his hand against the countries, and the land of Egypt shall not escape. He shall become ruler of the treasures of gold and of silver, and all the precious things of Egypt, and the Libyans and the Cushites shall follow in his train. [The treasures of Cleopatra were famous at that time.]

Verse 44: But news from the east and the north shall alarm him [At this point, the focus seems to shift specifically to Herod again. Reports from the east may refer to the Magi inquiring about the Christ child; meanwhile, reports from the north may refer to two of his sons in Rome who were plotting against him], and he shall go out with great fury to destroy and devote many to destruction. [Herod's "slaughter of the innocents" of Bethlehem in search of the Messiah at the infancy of Jesus; Herod also had three of his sons killed and murdered his wife; he killed three hundred army officers; he burned alive forty men who tore down the golden eagle over the temple gate; and he plotted to have all the leaders of the Jews killed upon his death so the people would mourn.]

Verse 45: And he shall pitch his palatial tents [Herod had palaces at Caesarea near the Mediterranean Sea, in Jerusalem, and at Jericho near the Dead Sea.] between the sea and the glorious holy mountain [or, perhaps, between the seas, i.e., the Mediterranean Sea and the Dead Sea and the glorious holy mountain]. Yet he shall come to his end, with none to help him. [As noted earlier, Herod died a terribly painful death, with no medical treatments able to help him.][3]

The Time of the End

Chapter 12 moves the vision beyond Herod the Great to focus on events later in the "time of the end."

"At that time shall arise Michael, the great prince who has charge of your people. And there shall be a time of trouble, such as never has been since there was a nation till that time. But at that time your people shall be delivered, everyone whose name shall be found written in the book. And many of those who sleep in the dust of the earth shall awake, some to everlasting life, and some to shame and everlasting contempt. And those who are wise shall shine like the brightness of the sky above; and those who turn many to righteousness, like the stars forever and ever. But you, Daniel, shut up the words and seal the book, until the time of the end. Many shall run to and fro, and knowledge shall increase."

Then I, Daniel, looked, and behold, two others stood, one on this bank of the stream and one on that bank of the stream. And someone said to the man clothed in linen, who was above the waters of the stream, "How long shall it be till the end of these wonders?" And I heard the man clothed in linen, who was above the waters of the stream; he raised his right hand and his left hand toward heaven and swore by him who lives forever that it would be for a time, times, and half a time, and that when the shattering of the power of the holy people comes to an end all these things would be finished. I heard, but I did not understand. Then I said, "O my lord, what shall be the outcome of these things?" He said, "Go your way, Daniel, for the words are shut up and sealed until the time of the end. Many shall purify themselves and make themselves white and be refined, but the wicked shall act wickedly. And none of the wicked shall understand, but those who are wise shall understand. And from the time that the regular burnt offering is taken away and the abomination that makes desolate is set up, there shall be 1,290 days. Blessed is he who waits and arrives at the 1,335 days. But go your way till the end. And you shall rest and shall stand in your allotted place at the end of the days."

—Daniel 12:1–13

Distress and Deliverance for God's People

Verse 1: At that time shall arise Michael, the great prince who has charge of your people. [Michael, the archangel who apparently has a special role in protecting God's people, was previously mentioned in Dan. 10:13, 21, and will be again in Jude 9 and Rev. 12:7. That he "shall arise" suggests his taking action, in this case to act on behalf of all those who, through faith in Jesus, both Jew and Gentile, are the true people of God, and against the "evil generation" of apostate Israel that rejected Jesus, put Him to death, and persecuted His followers. Cf. Matt. 12:39–45.] And there shall be a time of trouble, such as never has been since there was a nation till that time. [This is the "great tribulation" of Matt. 24:21, referring to the period of the Jewish revolt from AD 66–70. Due to the cumulative abominations perpetrated by the people of Israel, in Ezekiel 5:9 the Lord uses similar language in speaking of the horrors of the Babylonian conquest of Jerusalem.] But at that time your people shall be delivered, everyone whose name shall be found written in the book. [The context of this deliverance suggests it may be twofold: After the Romans crushed the Jewish revolt, the Jewish leaders were no longer in a position to actively persecute those Jews who had trusted in Jesus as the Messiah. Beyond this deliverance, however, is envisioned the greater ultimate deliverance to eternal life of both Jewish and Gentile Christians.]

Verse 2: And many of those who sleep in the dust of the earth shall awake, some to everlasting life, and some to shame and everlasting contempt. [Those who are characterized elsewhere in Scripture as being "asleep" in *sheol*, awaiting the resurrection, will now be resurrected to their eternal reality. This resurrection is further referenced in Matt. 27:52; John 5:25; 1 Cor.15:12–23, 51; and 1 Thess. 4:13–17. Perhaps it is noteworthy that here the focus is not on the punishment of those who will not have eternal life, but on their shame and everlasting contempt.]

Verse 3: And those who are wise shall shine like the brightness of the sky above; and those who turn many to righteousness, like the stars forever and ever. [Especially noteworthy are those who, as evangelists, pastors, and teachers—whether those are their formal roles or not—give themselves to sharing their knowledge of God and the good news of Jesus with the world around them.]

Final Instructions for Daniel

Daniel is told to "shut up the words and seal the book, until the time of the end" (Dan.12:4), and that "the words are shut up and sealed until the time of the end" (12:9). Although Daniel would write down his account of the visions, he himself should not be bothered any further with them, or proclaim them to his contemporaries, because the events described would occur far beyond his lifetime. Daniel's written record of these visions would be studied and recopied by faithful Jews through the centuries while the sequence of events being described was being fulfilled, until "the time of the end" would arrive. Any clearer understanding would need to wait for those who would see the unfolding of events at the coming of Christ and the change of covenant eras.

The reference to many who "shall run to and fro, and knowledge shall increase" is ambiguous, but certainly would include those who will proclaim the gospel to those who are in spiritual darkness (cf. Hos. 4:6; Acts 17:23–30; 2 Cor. 2:14). That "knowledge shall increase" should not be presumed to refer to the increase in knowledge in general, but rather, in the words from Habakkuk 2:14, that "the earth will be filled with the knowledge of the glory of the LORD as the waters cover the sea." The mustard seed of the kingdom of God continues to grow today as the gospel is proclaimed and lives are transformed to His glory.

How Long?

Daniel finds himself beside a river and overhears a conversation. Three others are involved—whether humans or angelic beings is initially unclear, though they are in human form. One is on each side of a stream. Another is clothed in linen and is "above the waters of the stream." Linen was the fabric of the priestly garments and is also worn by Christ in Revelation 19:14. The possibility that Daniel is seeing the pre-incarnate Christ here evokes a similar moment at the time of Jesus' transfiguration, when Jesus is seen to be talking with Moses and Elijah (Luke 9:30–31).

The figure in linen is asked, "How long shall it be till the end of these wonders?" The answer makes clear that the sense of the question is concerned with the "time of trouble" mentioned in 12:1. How long will this time of trouble last?

The answer is given as an oath, sworn by the man in linen above the river, "that it would be for a time, times, and half a time [apparently a year, two years, and half a year], and that when the shattering of the power of the holy people comes to an end all these things would be finished." This period of three and a half years would be from the invasion of Galilee by the Roman army under Vespasian in the spring of AD 67 to the destruction of the temple and the conquering and looting of Jerusalem in August/September AD 70. When Jerusalem was conquered and the temple was destroyed, the old covenant would be ended and all these prophecies would be fulfilled.

Daniel still does not understand everything that will happen. "O my lord, what shall be the outcome of these things?" he asks. First he is told that "the words are shut up and sealed until the time of the end." As in 12:4, again Daniel is told that the revelations to him have come to an end and will remain unclear until "the time of the end." (Note that here the words to Daniel are closed up and sealed—not understandable—for five hundred years until their fulfillment in the first century. In Revelation 22:10, by contrast, John is told instead *not* to seal up the words of Revelation because the time was near—to be fulfilled in large part only a few years later in the first century.)

The further answer to Daniel's question comes in two parts. First, there is the general assurance that many will be purified and refined and have understanding, pointing to the power of the Holy Spirit to transform our hearts and minds as we yield to His work in our lives. Yet wickedness and a willful lack of understanding will characterize others. Wickedness continues in our world, but as the gospel is proclaimed and people respond, the kingdom of God is growing, and those who trust in Jesus are being purified and refined.

The second part of the answer to Daniel is the more specific reminder of the predictions of Daniel 8 and 9 regarding the end of the daily temple sacrifices (Dan. 8:11–13) and the abomination that causes its desolation (Dan. 8:13; 9:27). The period of 1,290 days is suggested in Luke 21:20–21 and Matthew 24:15–16, which point to "the abomination that makes desolate" being at hand when the Roman armies under Cestius briefly besieged Jerusalem in November AD 66. Josephus reports that the cessation of the required daily sacrifices happened during the later Roman siege in July of AD 70. The longer period of 1,335 days reflects the blessing of those who would survive until the final Jerusalem resistance to the Romans ended in early September AD 70, after which Titus immediately extended clemency and freed those who had been imprisoned by the zealot gangs.[4]

The final words for Daniel, who is quite elderly at this point, offer him comfort. He will be able to rest and be assured that someday he will be resurrected and stand in the presence of his Lord and God.

ENDNOTES

Chapter 1

1. Biblical scholars who deny the possibility of predictive prophecy usually date the writing of Daniel in the period of the Maccabees and interpret the four successive kingdoms as the Babylonians, Medes, Persians, and Greeks. But for anyone accepting that God can reveal future events, the evidence in favor of the identities of these kingdoms as outlined here is overwhelming. See John S. Evans, *The Four Kingdoms of Daniel* (Maitland, FL: Xulon Press, 2004) for a comprehensive defense of the sequence ending with the Romans in both chapters 2 and 7. Also, evidence from the Dead Sea Scrolls would seem to point to the existence of the book of Daniel long before the second century BC. See Gerhard Hasel, "New Light on the Book of Daniel from the Dead Sea Scrolls," *Bible and Spade* (Spring 2011): 43–47.

2. Evans, 105–110.
3. Frank E. Gaebelein, Gleason L. Archer, Jr., Leon J. Wood, and Richard J. Patterson, *Expositor's Bible Commentary: Daniel and the Minor Prophets* (Grand Rapids, MI: Zondervan, 1985), 47.
4. Paul Johnson, *A History of the Jews* (New York: Harper and Row, 1987), 112; also, Evans, 123; and *Encyclopedia Judaica* (Jerusalem: Keter, 1994), 18:87.

Chapter 2

1. See, for example, John S. Evans, *The Four Kingdoms of Daniel* for a comprehensive defense of this understanding of the four beasts.
2. Compare Mark 13:26; 14:62; Matthew 16:27–28; 19:28; John 1:50; 3:13; 5:27; 9:35–39; and Revelation 1:13.
3. Josephus' list of Roman emperors is summarized in Evans, *Four Kingdoms*, 402.
4. A list of the Roman governors may be found at www.4enoch.org.
5. Alternatively, one would reach the same result by beginning with Julius Caesar and counting the rule of the Second Triumvirate as distinct from Augustus's imperial reign.
6. Flavius Josephus' *Jewish War* gives a full recounting of the Roman campaign under Vespasian. A modern translation with extensive commentary is: *Josephus: The Jewish War*, Gaalya Cornfeld, General Editor (Grand Rapids: Zondervan, 1982).
7. Solomon Grayzel, *A History of the Jews* (Philadelphia: Jewish Publication Society of America, 1947), 176.

8. Louis H. Feldman, "Financing the Coliseum," *Biblical Archaeology Review* (July/August 2001): 20–31, 60.

9. Ibid.

10. Josephus, *The Jewish War*, VII.5.148-162. Also as famously depicted on the Arch of Titus in Rome.

11. Ibid.

12. Shlomo Moussaieff, "The 'New Cleopatra' and the Jewish Tax," *Biblical Archaeology Review* (January/February 2010): 47–48; also in Cassius Dio, *Roman History*, trans. Earnest Cary (Cambridge, Mass.: Harvard University Press, 1925), Book LXV, 271.

13. As quoted by early church historian Eusebius of Caesarea. See *Eusebius: The Church History*, trans. Paul L. Maier (Grand Rapids: Kregel, 2007), 106.

Chapter 3

1. For details regarding the evil acts of Antiochus, see 2 Maccabees 5–6, also www.JewishEncyclopedia.com.

2. John E. Goldingay, *Word Biblical Commentary: Daniel* (Nashville: Nelson, 1989), 208.

3. For details regarding Herod the Great, see John S. Evans, *The Four Kingdoms of Daniel*, 250–260; and Paul L. Maier's *Eusebius: The Church History*, 39–42. For an analysis of Herod's health issues, see Nikos Kokkinos, "Herod's Death," *Biblical Archaeological Review* (March/April 2002): 28–35, 62.

Chapter 4

1. See, for example, Vern Poythress, "Hermeneutical Factors in Determining the Beginning of the Seventy

Weeks (Daniel 9:25)," *Trinity Journal*, 6 NS (1985): 131–149.

2. Josephus, in his *Antiquities of the Jews*, purports to quote from a letter from Cyrus in this regard. See Flavius Josephus, *The Works of Josephus*, trans. William Whiston (Peabody, Mass.: Hendrickson, 1987), 286.

3. See Philip Mauro, *The Wonders of Bible Chronology* (Ashburn, VA: Hess Publications, 2001), 7–9, 106–108. See also Martin Anstey, *Chronology of the Old Testament* (originally published in 1913 as *The Romance of Bible Chronology*) (Grand Rapids, MI: Kregel, 1973), 262ff.; and James Jordan, "The Capitulation of Biblical Chronology," *Biblical Chronology* 2, no. 1 (January 1990); and James Jordan, "Daniel's 70 Weeks," *Biblical Chronology* 2, no. 12 (December 1990).

4. See Martin Anstey, *Romance of Bible Chronology*, 1913, reprinted in preteristarchive.com; and James Jordan, "The Chronology of Ezra and Nehemiah (III)," *Biblical Chronology* 3, no. 4 (April 1991).

5. E. J. Bickerman, *Chronology of the Ancient World* (London: Thames and Hudson, 1980), 89.

6. Eusebius, *Proof of the Gospel*, trans. W.J. Ferrar (New York: Macmillan, 1920), Book VIII, chap.2, 395–396, accessed at www.preteristarchive.com/church history/0312_eusebius_proof.html.

7. Beyond the evidence of the Biblical accounts of messianic expectations and false messiahs of that period, see Roger Beckwith, "Daniel 9 and the Date of Messiah's Coming in Essene, Hellenistic, Pharisaic, Zealot and Early Christian Computation," *Revue de Qumran* 10 (December 1981): 521–542.

8. Alternatively, it is noteworthy that the early church historian Eusebius is quoted by Jerome as saying that the prevalent view of the early church was that each year of the 70th week of Daniel represented a ten-year period. "This same Eusebius reports another view as well, which I do not entirely reject, that most authorities extend the one (last) week of years to the sum of seventy years, reckoning each year as a ten-year period," beginning with the birth of Jesus, having His public ministry, death and resurrection at the mid-point, and concluding with the Jewish revolt and destruction of the Temple at its end. See Jerome, *Jerome's Commentary on Daniel*, trans. Gleason L. Archer, Jr. (Grand Rapids: Baker Book House, 1958), 103.

Chapter 5

1. These explanatory notes are taken in large part from those given in the NIV *Study Bible* (Grand Rapids: Zondervan, 1985) and reflect the consensus from various sources. "Both liberal and conservative scholars agree that all of chapter 11 up to this point contains strikingly accurate predictions of the whole sweep of historical events from the reign of Cyrus ... to the unsuccessful effort of Antiochus Epiphanes to stamp out the Jewish faith" (Gaebelein, et al, *Expositor's Bible Commentary, Daniel and the Minor Prophets*, 143).
2. Josephus, *The Jewish War*, I, 21, 1–8.
3. Kokkinos, "Herod's Death," 28–35, 62.
4. Josephus, *Jewish Wars*, VI, 2,1 and 4,8; IX,1.

REDEMPTION◗PRESS